LIVING BY THE OCEAN

LIVING BY THE OCEAN

CONTEMPORARY HOUSES BY THE SEA

The importance of the ocean to humankind, and the power it has on our imagination, cannot be overstated. It has always been a rich source of natural resources and sustenance. In our evolutionary story and countless creation myths, the sea is a key protagonist. It also holds a beguiling sense of mystery; the surfaces of the Moon, Mars, and Venus are more accurately mapped than the world's ocean floors. Little wonder, then, that many of us want to live by it.

The ocean we gaze at today does not, to our minds, appear different from that seen by our ancestors. Stretching beyond the horizon, it offers a glimpse of the seemingly infinite; when calm, its vastness has a meditative quality. Here we can let our minds settle, forget the minutiae of everyday life, and be cradled by its gentle rhythmic sounds.

However, the ocean is in constant flux. It can be wild and unpredictable, the site and cause of natural disaster: shipwreck, tsunami, flooding, volcanic eruption, and earthquake. This restlessness and danger are equally compelling, transforming the sea into a thrilling theater of untamed beauty.

This book explores architecture that celebrates all of the sea's paradoxical qualities. From Oceania to South America, Europe to Asia, here are fifty of the world's best contemporary coastal houses, divided into three distinct groups. The first seeks the ultimate sensory experience of being surrounded by the sea, whether on islands or narrow peninsulas or even partially submerged in the water. The second group stands in apparent defiance of rugged and challenging locations: plunging cliffs, isolated coasts, or harsh climates. The final group is drawn to gentler waters, openly embracing the sea from the relative safety of rolling dunes, sandy beaches, and sheltered harbors.

In designing these houses, the architects have been mindful to make as little impact as possible on the fragile coastal environments. With disturbing images of plastic islands seared into our consciousness and global warming continuing apace, sustainability is a critically important focus. Many of these residences have light footprints, employ recycled and local materials, adopt eco-friendly vernacular building techniques, and rely on natural ventilation and abundant solar and geothermal energy. Some are designed to evolve through various iterations; several are adaptive reuse projects rather than houses built from scratch; yet all are built to last.

Building a house by the ocean is seldom an easy task. It can be fraught with risks: landscapes can be inhospitable or locations hard to reach, cliffs pose engineering challenges, and flooding and erosion present a constant threat. Coastal homes are frequently under siege from strong winds, rain, and punishing sun. Despite such factors, the examples in this book show that it is, undoubtedly, worth all the effort.

Life's one certainty is its impermanence, and perhaps this is why we often find solace in the sea's perpetual state of change; its uncontrollable nature and impenetrable depths can make our own lives seem more manageable. A house by the ocean can offer many things: a place to reflect, unwind, awaken our senses, be thrilled or humbled. It is much more than a place to stay—it is somewhere to feel truly alive.

[1] BUILT WITHIN THE OCEAN

On islands, on narrow peninsulas, or—in two daring cases—partly submerged in the water itself, the houses in this chapter are surrounded by the ocean. They may be humble or extravagant, serene or dramatic, but there's one quality these dwellings all share: a sense of detachment, isolation even, that can be quite magical.

These homes are designed to pull their inhabitants into sensory worlds; the pleasures are not simply visual, although the outlooks are invariably beautiful. The designs immerse residents in the scent and taste of salty seawater, and the ever-changing sounds of the waves, from gentle lapping to deafening roar. These houses are close enough to the sea to allow the sensation of sand between the toes and water overhead to be a regular privilege. Interiors feature unobstructed outlooks, open and uncluttered layouts, and minimal decoration—all strategies to draw the inhabitants' attention outward, toward the marine light and the horizon.

Often in commanding positions on cliffs or hillsides, the homes in this chapter strike a balance between blending in and using bold forms to create a strong visual identity. Depending on the quality of light, the corrugated-aluminum cladding of a diminutive Scottish dwelling signals its presence through reflections, or flattens to the slate gray of a stormy sky and sea. Differences in scale matter: massive views juxtapose with thoughtful detailing and painstaking craftsmanship, both inside and out. Nature is omnipresent or actively encouraged to encroach; in one horseshoe-shaped Greek house embedded into a hillside, it is hard to tell where the building ends and the landscape begins. That house is designed to heal its surroundings, with earth from its excavation used to repair scarring from the construction of old, now disused roads.

Two abodes with underwater rooms—one relatively modest, the other inspired by the opulence of first-class air travel—demonstrate remarkable technical prowess to create womblike, immersive spaces in which to connect with the abyss. The psychological and physical experience of being so close to the water is thrilling, and the relationship between these spaces and the ocean could not be more intimate.

Yuji Yamazaki Architecture
THE MURAKA
2018 | Rangali Island, Maldives

Probably nowhere else in the world quite matches the experience of staying at the Muraka: part luxury yacht, part underwater boudoir, the villa resembles a set from a spy movie. Arriving on Conrad Maldives Rangali Island by private seaplane, guests access the property via a long jetty. The svelte, spacious upper story contains an open-plan kitchen, living, and dining area, main bedroom, and two further bedrooms—as well as a gym, if things become too laid-back. Guests can sunbathe on a spacious outdoor terrace, from which they can plunge directly into the sea.

The submerged lower level, reached by spiral staircase or elevator, contains a bedroom, a bathroom, a lounge, and ample storage. The bed is positioned under a projecting domed section with 7-inch (18-centimeter) -thick acrylic walls, through which guests can marvel at the abundant Maldivian sea life—but there are plenty of other views to be had from the lounge and even the bathroom. The villa was prefabricated in three parts, transported by barge to the site and welded together, then craned into place with divers on hand to guide it into place, and finally secured onto concrete piles. With an aesthetic inspired by first-class air travel, the interior decor upstairs is crisp, modern, and bright, while below sea level it is moodier and more opulent. Unsurprisingly, a night here comes at quite a price.

Aesop.

Desciencelab
MONTAUK HOUSE
2018 | Montauk, NY, USA

Nestling amid wetlands, this vacation home on the tip of a Long Island peninsula is almost entirely surrounded by water, with a bay to the north and the Atlantic to the south. The residence was originally a two-story clapboard home with badly planned, tight interiors and an exterior that featured a mishmash of architectural styles. Brooklyn, New York–based studio, Desciencelab, which specializes in architectural millwork, was given the task of designing and constructing a top-to-bottom makeover, in which only the overall structure and the position of all openings were retained. The result is akin to a sleek, finely crafted boathouse.

To boost visual coherence, Desciencelab ripped off the clapboards and clad the entire exterior in narrow horizontal strips of meranti wood, commonly used in boatbuilding. The studio also shifted an exterior staircase to one end of the house, so as not to break up the facade, and fitted the balcony with cable railings to open up views of the water. Using contrasting black metal frames on the windows and doors created a sharper, more defined presence.

Desciencelab completely refreshed the interiors as well. Removing a second-floor fireplace and central spiral staircase created a spacious living and dining area, while white pine flooring and custom-made teak cabinetry brought a precise, crisp finish. The project has transformed the house from a cluttered, awkward space into a tranquil, well-planned home, perfectly suited to its coastal environment.

Amelia Tavella Architectes
CASA SANTA TERESA
2020 | Ajaccio, Corsica, France

This 1950s villa has been transformed from near ruin to a chic, contemporary vacation home. Occupying a commanding hillside plot above a beach in Ajaccio, the capital city of Corsica, the residence was run down and close to being engulfed by vegetation. Local architect Amelia Tavella and her eponymous firm designed a total renovation of the four-story house, removing numerous internal walls to open up coastal views and improve the flow between rooms. The resulting arrangement comprises four bedrooms spread over two floors, plus a suite under the roof eaves, and terraces across three levels. To honor the house's history, the firm retained original midcentury features, such as the zigzagging metal balustrades and white cinder-block walls around the garden. Nature is welcomed in: the tops of palm trees are visible from the second-floor living room, and outdoor areas are fringed with greenery.

Exterior spaces are a natural focus when designing in a warm climate, but here the interiors were given equally careful attention. The vast living room is flooded with Mediterranean light, and nothing obstructs its interior and exterior views; doors have been replaced by simple open archways, and glazed panels pivot open to access the balcony. For the furnishings, Tavella also chose items for their lightness and transparency, such as the cane-and-rattan Chandigarh chairs by Pierre Jeanneret and woven lampshades. The soothing palette features a blend of white walls and warm, umber-toned timber, enlivened by pops of orange and turquoise, the quintessential colors of a Matisse painting.

This bold and imaginative summer home is wedged into a craggy outcrop in Kárpathos, one of the Greek Dodecanese islands. Instead of trying to mimic the landscape or blend in with it, Patio House complements its environment while retaining its own sense of identity. The concrete oblong box cantilevers out over the hillside, playing cleverly with ideas of void and volume, inside and outside. The focal point of the design is a large interior courtyard with a garden: a sheltered green area to eat, relax, and socialize. A terrace integrated into one corner of the house is wrapped with a concrete shell that acts as a buffer against the strong local winds but is pierced with apertures that frame views out to sea and along the coast. Throughout the residence, there is a sense of being indoors when one is outdoors, protected from, yet exposed to, the elements. Away from the house, another outdoor space is accessed via a staircase leading to a plateau below, where a covered dining area with spectacular sea views waits to be discovered.

The house is constructed of board-formed concrete, which provides a man-made contrast with the rocks it perches on but retains an organic feel and will weather naturally over time. Timber window frames, clay brick patios in the courtyard, and terra-cotta tiles in the bathroom add warmth to the materials palette. Elsewhere, the crisp interiors feel natural, fresh, and bright.

1100 Architect

HOUSE ON IKEMA ISLAND

2016 | Ikema Island, Japan

With a design that is composed yet understated, this house cantilevers over rocky terrain on a bluff overlooking the East China Sea. Located on Ikema, an island midway between Okinawa and Taiwan, the home combines a minimalist contemporary aesthetic with more traditional architectural features. Its pale concrete facade harmonizes perfectly with the color of the rocks, while the smooth slab roof provides a striking contrast with their uneven and broken forms. The house is fully glazed on two sides—those facing the swimming pool and the sea—while the other two, including the street-facing elevation, are almost completely windowless to ensure privacy. When the owners are away, the glass facades can be fully concealed behind sliding aluminum shutters, which unfold from a cypress box on the exterior.

Raised on pillars above a concrete plinth, the house takes full advantage of the coastal views. On the first floor, the main living area comprises an open-plan kitchen, dining room, and lounge overlooking the sea, while two bedrooms are tucked away at the more enclosed end. Like many Japanese houses, there are also two tatami rooms, one of which contains a Buddhist family altar, known as a butsudan, and the other a tokonoma, a niche for displaying art. Other traditional Japanese architectural elements include sliding translucent shoji walls and cypress paneling. With its simple, uncluttered design, the house maintains a strong but calming visual presence on the cliff.

Nestled among ranks of white, flat-roofed houses, this compact dwelling comprising two self-contained apartments is perched high up in the cliffs of Imerovigli, a village on Santorini, one of the Greek Cyclades islands. The building—like many of its neighbors—is carved into the rock face: its side-by-side apartments occupy deep, cavelike spaces, minimally decorated to create an atmosphere of calm and reflection.

Each apartment is reached via its own external staircase, which descends from a shared roof terrace at street level. The larger unit has two en suite bedrooms, while the other smaller unit has one; both spaces have private balconies from which to enjoy Santorini's world-famous sunsets. Since the sea is far below, to give respite from summer heat, each apartment has a crystalline plunge pool, which appears to be sculpted from the foundations of the building: the smaller apartment's is inside, though a permanent opening in the external wall admits sunlight and frames views of other nearby islands; the larger apartment's flows from inside to outside, opening up panoramic views of the Aegean Sea. The subterranean rooms, with their vaulted ceilings, are cool but not dark. Softly undulating interior walls are painted a pale fawn—a warm tone to contrast with the traditional dazzling white of the exterior. Circular or arched internal openings and furniture with rounded forms offset the building's sharp, clean, cubic external lines. What could, in the wrong hands, be cramped dark hideaways are instead beguiling, immersive spaces, meticulously finished both inside and out.

MANTA UNDERWATER ROOM

2013 | Pemba Island, Tanzania

In the Underwater Room, guests can spend a night mesmerized by shoals of colorful fish, 13 feet (4 meters) below the surface of the Indian Ocean. Africa's first underwater hotel suite is part of the Manta Resort, which lies within a conservation area on Pemba Island in Tanzania's Zanzibar archipelago. Its structure and concept are surprisingly simple: above sea level is a covered outdoor lounge area and enclosed bathroom clad in local hardwood; this supports a generous roof deck for sunbathing and stargazing; and attached below the surface is a cuboid glass bedroom, anchored to the ocean floor with cables (cable tethers were chosen to secure the suite rather than placing it on seabed supports because the strong local tides and currents would have caused too much wear and tear). Facilities are minimal but adequate for overnight stays. Guests arrive by boat and enter the undersea pod by a flight of stairs leading from the upper deck. Once submerged, they can enjoy captivating 360-degree views of the ocean surroundings, which are spotlit at night, creating a magnet for curious rays, squid, and octopuses. The light at this time also provides a haven for certain species from predators; this in conjunction with the conservation area's no-netting policy has supported the proliferation of over 200 species and the regeneration of the coral reef. Swedish artist and entrepreneur Mikael Genberg, the mastermind of the operation, has since set his sights on building a house on the moon.

PENINSULA HOUSE

2018 | Kanto, Japan

At first glance, Peninsula House looks simple, almost purely utilitarian, appearing as two rectangular volumes arranged at right angles. Yet one corner of its structure rests on a massive stepped slope, which descends beneath and laterally beyond the building's longest arm, supported by just a single round pillar. This design has a huge impact, expressing weight and lightness simultaneously and creating a striking silhouette; the dramatic concrete staircase might suggest a wave or a mountain.

Occupying a strip of land that juts out from a small fishing harbor, the four-bedroom house is designed to be a year-round retreat. It turns its back on the strong northwesterly winds that blow in the winter, yet welcomes in a cooling southeastern breeze in summer. Rough board-formed concrete on the exterior makes a strong visual connection with the rocky cliffs nearby, while smooth, pale concrete floor slabs create an almost seamless surface between first-floor living-dining area and the large terrace. The living area occupies an impressive double-height space, with views over the sea and of Mount Fuji. Also on this level are two bedrooms, as well as a gym and bathroom with more sea views. An open wooden staircase leads to the second floor, where there is a study, two more bedrooms, and another terrace. Built with both functionality and family needs in mind, Peninsula House is nevertheless a daring building that wants to make its presence felt.

Raad Studio
BEACH HOUSE
2018 | Sea Bright, NJ, USA

Creating a strong connection with the dune landscape and achieving good flood protection were both key priorities in the design of this New Jersey beachside home. Located on a spit of land bordered by the Atlantic on one side and the Navesink River on the other, the area sees storms and high rainfall during the area's humid summers, making it vulnerable to coastal flooding. The beach's original dunes were long gone, so a network of supporting concrete walls and piers was built to raise the house above the historic high watermark, between which sand was added to create new dunes. Penetrations in the dunes allow water to sluice through, and a path running beneath the house, between two concrete retaining walls, also serves to channel off excess rainwater.

The clean, sharp lines of the three-bedroom home demonstrate outstanding craftsmanship using timber from native North American species: the exterior cladding is Alaskan yellow cedar, which will weather naturally. The house's luminous, amply glazed interiors are softened by a relaxed decor in soothing colors. In keeping with its context, the design incorporated local maritime construction techniques, such as the wood pile systems used in nearby dock buildings and decking made of ipe, a strong timber often used by the industry due to its good traction in wet weather. The different-sized stacked volumes allow for a spacious roof terrace for hot summers, and when the weather turns, Beach House becomes a perfect lookout for storm watching.

DECA Architecture
RING HOUSE
2016 | Agia Galini, Crete, Greece

Ring House is an example of how coastal architecture can be supremely in tune with its environment. The low-profile two-story residence, built in the shape of a horseshoe from local Cretan stone, wraps around a hillside and then reaches up the slope behind it to pull a sizable grove of olive trees into its plot. The upper floor contains living spaces and bedrooms, glazed on both sides to allow light to penetrate; additional shuttered bedrooms are housed in the lower floor. A flat roof fitted with solar panels runs the length of the building; overhanging and pierced at both ends, it provides partially shaded, open-air areas for a terrace with pool and carport, respectively. Within the curve of the horseshoe lies a sheltered interior garden filled with citrus trees, thyme, and grasses.

A key element of the house's concept was for it to have an active healing effect on the land. A network of old roads and the construction needed to build them had caused scarring on the hillside, so as the site was cleared, excavated earth was used to cover over these gouged-out routes. To further restore the land, seeds from native plants were collected locally, cultivated in a greenhouse, and sown in the newly laid earth. Because nothing like this house had been built locally before, the architects interviewed more than fifty craftspeople before appointing a team.

SEA FRONT VILLA

2019 | Okinawa, Japan

The strength of this Japanese weekend house is its relentless purity of form. A monumental white object, it makes no attempt to blend into the landscape at all: it presents itself more as a sculpture framed by vegetation, sky, water, and sand. The single-story house's site was raised to ensure better views and privacy from the road beneath it, and the beach is a stone's throw beyond a dense strip of greenery.

The home's broad open-plan kitchen, living, and dining space opens up onto a vast north-facing terrace with an infinity pool and a gigantic water feature—a long, shallow basin into which water flows constantly, its splashing sounds a calming soundtrack for sunbathing. Both the pool and water basin connect visually with the sea beyond, their reflections of the sky and mirroring of the sea seeming to expand the spatial boundaries of the home. Monolithic white walls at either end of the terrace offer privacy, shade, and shelter from wind but also add to the house's radically simple geometry. Four identical, almost monastic bedrooms overlook the terrace. They are simply places to sleep—the indoor and outdoor living areas are the priority. The villa's entirely windowless south-facing facade ensures protection from direct sun. Inside, white furniture, the palest wood flooring, and minimal ornament keep this a restful, meditative space.

Office of McFarlane Biggar Architects + Designers

BOWEN ISLAND HOUSE

2020 | Bowen Island, BC, Canada

With its beauty and proximity to Vancouver, Bowen Island is a popular weekend destination in the middle of Howe Sound. The clients for this family home wanted a house that was designed in harmony with its natural surroundings. Amid evergreen trees and ferns, and tucked beneath towering cliffs, the slender two-story building is positioned perpendicular to the sound, giving it a gentle visual presence from land and sea. Stepping down the slope, the north-facing dwelling receives light from the east and west, and is further illuminated by light wells on its green roof.

The narrow rectangular design gives the house a light footprint and made construction in the remote location more straightforward. The home is able to operate off the grid during extreme weather, powered by its own generator, while fresh water is provided by a private well. Energy use is low due to its compact size—yet it comfortably accommodates three bedrooms, two bathrooms, and an open-plan living area. A cast-in-place concrete base makes a strong visual connection with the rocky terrain, while the upper story's black-stained cedar paneling helps the house blend into the dense forest. A contrastingly bright interior is clad with locally sourced pale hemlock wood. Expansive views of the sound from communal areas and the main bedroom alternate with narrower, more fleeting glimpses elsewhere, but the forest and sea remain a constant presence. In every sense, the house balances thoughtful restraint with a wholehearted embrace of its sublime island context.

FIRE ISLAND HOUSE

2012 | Fire Island, NY, USA

A slender barrier island south of Long Island, unspoiled Fire Island is one of New York's go-to vacation spots, offering miles of blissful, car-free shoreline to while away the summers. However, its exposed location leaves it vulnerable to the elements. Storms barrel in from the Atlantic in winter, battering properties with wind, rain, and sea spray. Not one to shy away from such challenges, the firm Delson or Sherman Architects renovated this family beach house to expand it, strengthen its storm protection, and create a more fluid connection between indoors and outdoors. The architects added a new wing upstairs for additional bedrooms and bathrooms. They also reconfigured the downstairs kitchen, dining, and living area to improve access to a new raised deck with a pool. A covered porch overlooking the beach provides a sheltered outdoor spot for dining. To hurricane-proof the home, the architects used white concrete cladding, rustproof metal roofing, and reinforced glass. Soon after the renovation, a true test came when Hurricane Sandy hit the island—the house survived undamaged. The new uncluttered facade, punctuated with simple rectangular openings, complements the Modernist designs of much of the island's architecture. Sloping roofs lend a sense of tentlike protection; they also echo the form of the dune on which the house is built. In keeping with the beach-house aesthetic, interiors are clad in whitewashed pine, and exposed ceiling beams bring a touch of rustic charm. Midcentury furniture with pops of color adds warmth and cheer on cold days.

TINHOUSE

2016 | Milovaig, Skye, Scotland, UK

Tucked into a hillside overlooking the Minch, the body of water separating Scotland's Inner and Outer Hebrides, this one-bedroom vacation retreat is a triumph of low-cost coastal design. It is the brainchild of Rural Design Architects founders Gill Smith and Alan Dickson, who also built the house by hand. A simple single-story pitched-roof dwelling, Tinhouse references the agricultural buildings common to Skye. The island light dances across the building's corrugated-aluminum cladding, the colors on its surface shifting continuously between slate gray and pale silver.

The climate can be unforgiving in this part of Scotland, so to retain heat, the mountain-facing south side and east end of the house are windowless. On the water-facing north side, a ribbon of glazing framing sea and mountain views runs the length of the building, wrapping around the west end. Pale gray concrete flooring and white-painted timber cladding keep the interiors bright, and splashes of warmth are added through orange, yellow, and pink textiles in the lounge and a two-tone blue kitchen wall. Low-cost or recycled materials were used wherever possible, such as plywood for drawers and kitchen units, and unused structural timber for the bed and seats. A clever and sustainable take on a coastal cabin, Tinhouse's rustic-meets-industrial aesthetic works perfectly in this remote landscape.

Patterson Associates Architects
NAISOSO ISLAND
2018 | Naisoso Island, Fiji

This house looks like a fantasy vacation retreat, but it is actually a pragmatic home that is designed to accommodate extended family gatherings. Located on Naisoso Island in Fiji's archipelago, it was built for a local couple who both work overseas and who wanted a house with a contemporary tropical aesthetic. The residence borrows certain features from Fiji's vernacular architecture: it is built of concrete to be cyclone-proof, painted white, and has different indoor and outdoor spaces for eating meals with family and friends. Expansive roof overhangs mean people can sit outside even when it is raining. The aluminum fins on the facade that give the house such an ultramodern look serve to ventilate and shade the interior. They also act as a security feature, closing tightly when the owners are away.

To protect it from future rises in sea level, the site was compacted and built up before the house was constructed, and a berm was built across the beachfront. The aluminum fins and joinery were imported, but the rest of the materials, such as concrete and timber, were low cost and locally sourced. Inside, there is a cinema room clad in dark wood, a three-bedroom guest suite, and five more bedrooms. In the living room, a freestanding coral stone wall adds organic texture to the otherwise sleek concrete interior.

[2] BUILT TO CONFRONT THE OCEAN

The ocean cannot be tamed, but for many, it is precisely this wild and wondrous energy that is so alluring. Located in dramatic outposts where the waves are big, the rocks sharp, and the weather unpredictable, the houses in this chapter are built to confront the sublime, all-consuming power of the sea. Unintimidated by seemingly inhospitable environments, they inhabit soaring cliffs, barren shingle beaches, or perches overlooking dangerous straits.

These are defiant houses: they meet the ocean head-on. A converted lighthouse in England, once a beacon of safety for those contending with the North Sea, is now a different kind of haven—a charming weekend getaway standing in proud recognition of its nautical past. Elsewhere, a cabin on a remote Arctic fjord, a former British radar station, and a concrete monolith on the rugged Chilean coast are some other examples that rise to the challenge. With a certain fearlessness, they stand like sentinels at land's end.

Some are dug into cliff faces or buried deep in turf; others are braced on rocky precipices like fortresses ready for battle. Often the houses have low, horizontal shapes, unobtrusive in the landscape and sturdy against wind and rain, yet others take more extroverted vertical forms, their block-like volumes cascading toward the ocean. Views are still all-important, but these structures must offer protection as well, and many include sheltered terraces and courtyard gardens.

Sometimes sourced from the site itself, materials must be robust enough to withstand extreme conditions. Concrete, used in several dwellings here, is tough and weather-resistant; it also echoes the materiality of surrounding rocks and can be molded into bold, monumental forms. Stone is an obvious natural choice, used for its sturdiness and raw beauty. Elsewhere, timber has been selected for its warm tactility and tendency to weather like driftwood. Needless to say, the standards of craftsmanship are high—they have to be for homes in these places to survive. Such designs are a gutsy response to the ocean's challenges, made possible by an exacting combination of engineering ingenuity, understated beauty, and true respect for nature.

This intriguing narrow concrete house on Chile's wild Coliumo peninsula juts out like a wall from the cliffside. Its Concepción-based architects, Mauricio Pezo and Sofía von Ellrichshausen, describe Loba House as a "cottage" because of its diminutive size. Constructed mostly of board-formed concrete, it is more of a sculpture to be lived in than a traditional dwelling.

The house is one story high but inside has a series of six stepped platforms following the slope of the cliff—essentially a large staircase. The top three levels are used as sleeping areas, while the lower spaces are used for cooking, dining, and relaxing. Storage is tucked under the platforms to keep the space clutter-free. A bathroom, kitchen area, and hearth are cleverly concealed within the hefty columns that support the ceiling, and the roof can be accessed from the hillside for use as a terrace. Three round skylights cut in the roof bring in light; additional crescent-shaped apertures in the walls provide another light source, casting sunlight into the building at certain times of day, and allow the sound of the sea to echo through the house. Loba House's rawness, openness to nature, and profound materiality make this an reflective, almost primal place in which to commune with the elements.

CABIN IN LYNGEN ALPS

2015 | Ravika, Norway

Taking the flattened and simplified form of a mountain, this Arctic wilderness cabin nestles into a crag overlooking a dark sand beach and the Lyngen fjord, east of the Norwegian city of Tromsö. Despite the design's low profile and reliance on natural materials—such as cedar cladding that blends in with surrounding stone, vegetation, and snow—the cabin still cuts a striking form amid the landscape.

During the design process, the architects considered a number of factors regarding the terrain, plot, sun's position during the day—and night in summertime—wind direction, heather and stone formations, and, perhaps most importantly, how best to achieve panoramic views of the sea and mountains. To this end, the cabin's front section, containing kitchen, living, and dining areas, is more rectangular in form, allowing a long stretch of floor-to-ceiling glass. To the rear, where the bedrooms are located, sloping walls give the cabin a strong sense of hunkering down. The main bedroom, however, angles away from the house to access dramatic mountain views; an adjacent sauna opens out to a deck with hot tub—or, for the courageous, the snow. To maintain focus on the views, interiors are simple, almost monastic, and the floors and ceilings are clad with a pale oak that bounces light around the spaces. Yet when the long Arctic winters draw in, geothermal energy and underfloor hydronic heating keep the cabin warm and homey.

Auhaus Architecture

CLIFF HOUSE

2019 | Ocean Grove, VIC, Australia

Cliff House breathes new life into a beautiful but tricky location for a beachside property. Overlooking the Bass Strait, it replaces a previous home belonging to the same owners that had taken a beating from strong southwesterly winds, sea spray, and driving rain. The project brief was for a stylish new residence that could stand up to these conditions and provide flexible, multigenerational spaces.

The structure is built from durable concrete, and sections of the facade are clad in hardwood timber, oil coated for protection, which will weather over time to blend in with the dunes and scrub. Built over three stories, the collection of volumes is grouped around a courtyard that has been elevated to midlevel to create a sheltered, intimate space. Away from the winds, the courtyard still enjoys uninterrupted sea views and features a swimming pool enclosed by a raised plant bed. The main bedroom is on the top floor; living areas with ocean views are on the first floor; and the basement level comprises a self-contained apartment for the owner's grandparents and a painting studio. Across the courtyard is a separate guest wing with two bedrooms, a lounge, and a bathroom. A palette of ocean greens and blues pervades the decor. Concrete is softened by furniture upholstered in luxurious textiles, such as velvet, and timber ceilings make the spaces feel warm and cocooned. The overall effect is sharp, contemporary, and relaxing.

Studio Mackereth
THE LIGHTHOUSE
2012 | Winterton-on-Sea, England, UK

When architect Sally Mackereth, of London-based Studio Mackereth, spotted this lighthouse for sale in Norfolk, England, it was a simple cylindrical tower with a flat concrete roof. Dating back to the eighteenth century, it has a mention in Daniel Defoe's 1719 novel *Robinson Crusoe*. Although habitable, the lighthouse was in a run-down state and needed major upgrading. It was also missing its lantern, which had been replaced by a concrete lid to be used by soldiers as a lookout post during World War II.

Seeing its potential as a weekend getaway, Mackereth snapped it up, adding a single-story glass-and-timber extension with a spacious kitchen-dining area and bathroom. She left the tower itself, with 3-foot (1-meter) -thick tapering walls, structurally unchanged, but made the space more suitable for family vacations. Mackereth converted the first floor into a small living room and sleeping area; the second floor, a kids' bunk room; the third, an adults' bedroom; and the fourth, a library with pull-down bed. She designed new curving furniture, including kitchen units, a leather banquette, and bunk beds, but retained the original stone floors. Finally, in an inspired touch, Mackereth created an entirely new floor at the top of the building, comprising a glass-walled lantern with a domed roof, which contains a second living room and mezzanine sleeping area. The lantern offers 360-degree views of the beach, the Norfolk countryside, and the North Sea. Breathing life into a historic building, this project created an enchanting seaside refuge for children and adults alike.

DESCEND
STAIRS
BACKWARDS

LIGHT

CASA GHAT

2016 | Cachagua, Chile

Rejecting coastal architecture's typical horizontality, Casa Ghat exploits its steep topography to create bold concrete forms that cascade thrillingly down a twenty-five-degree cliff face in the town of Cachagua, two hours north of Santiago, Chile. Taking its name from the Indian stone platforms that descend toward riversides, the home's unifying structure is its stepped roof supported by fifteen columns of varying sizes and shapes. The organic, treelike supports frame myriad vistas of the cliffs and seascape below.

The main bedroom is housed in a wood-clad rectangular volume that laterally pierces the roof and opens out onto a terrace, which connects to the base of a giant external staircase. This expansive outdoor area can also be accessed via a neighboring timber-clad volume containing a smaller internal staircase. More bedrooms are housed in a separate wing at the top rear of the property. A labyrinth of concrete staircases is also used to connect the interior, including a central, oversize one that flows down to the kitchen, living, and dining area on the lowest level, which is encased in panoramic glazing. Architect Max Núñez's innovative design allows for a series of complex spaces and views to unfold: ever-shifting vignettes broken up by the home's raw internal structure. Casa Ghat's daring concept, sculptural shapes, and sheer drama make for an impressive and highly unusual ocean residence.

Guz Architects

LOGIE POINT HOUSE

2018 | St Brelade, Jersey, UK

Logie Point is a wild, windswept location on a headland of Jersey, one of the Channel Islands. Consisting of a main house and a smaller house, the development was designed by Singapore-based British architect Guz Wilkinson, whose primary objective was to merge the main dwelling with the landscape as much as possible. The land appears to flow over the house so that when approached at ground level, the residence seems to be a one-story building: a series of interconnecting spaces that forms a horseshoe shape around a sheltered courtyard garden with a natural pond.

Viewed from the sea, however, the true scale of the house is revealed: it is a broadly reaching two-story building with floor-to-ceiling glazing on both levels. One enters at the second floor via a spectacular lobby with an undulating skylight. Just beyond this is a slender main living room focused on views of the sea, the heart of the house. A swooping wood-and-metal staircase descends to the family room below. Bedrooms and bathrooms are off to the sides, reached by cloister-like glazed corridors. Inside and outside the home, the abundant use of stone and wood creates a feeling of solidity and presence while tying the property to the Jersey landscape; curved metal roof overhangs add a sense of lightness and elegance. A truly elemental place to live, Logie Point House fuses with the earth and opens to the sea.

Perched on a craggy sandstone bluff above the Pacific Ocean, Bangalley Headland House could not be more different from the house it replaces—a pink Tuscan-style villa. In their brief to the architects, the clients requested something subtler that would make optimal use of the site, respect its natural surroundings, and possess a certain timelessness.

Nestling among boulders, Norfolk pines, and bushland, the three-story house comprises five staggered, linked pavilions arranged around the contours of the hillside. Guest rooms are dug into the cliff at the lowest level; the first-floor garden level is designed for dining and relaxing; and the top floor houses the main bedroom. Views of the ocean to the south and of Avalon Beach to the west are maximized throughout. But it is the materials and detailing that connect this house so perfectly with its environment. Cantilevering terraces and balconies, and projecting window hoods mirror the cliff's layered geology, as do the smoky-gray-and-black-brick exterior walls. The interiors are all about contrast and combination; luminous white brick walls are matched with polished stone floors, pale gray concrete roof beams, and vaulted ceilings clad in dark timber. Brass, used for balcony railings and a sculptural screen lining the staircase in the living room, adds a touch of warmth and opulence. Bangalley Headland House undoubtedly exudes style, but its sensitivity to the landscape lends it a sense of permanence and gravitas befitting of its privileged clifftop location.

Patterson Associates Architects

SCRUBBY BAY HOUSE

2014 | Banks Peninsula, New Zealand

The remote location of Scrubby Bay House is breathtaking—in a valley within a coastal sheep-and-cattle station, the residence overlooks an unspoiled beach with rolling, thundering surf. The house is designed for family groups who want an authentic New Zealand farm experience. Patterson Associates Architects understood that to compete with such a pristine landscape would be pointless. Instead, the design takes the form of the archetypal rural hut, combining two staggered pitched-roof volumes that exist in harmony with the impressive backdrop. The cedar exterior cladding and roof blend perfectly with the sun-bleached grass of the surrounding meadows and will gradually weather to the color of driftwood.

The far-from-spartan interior is fitted out floor to ceiling with locally sourced macrocarpa wood paired with black steel fittings; doorknobs, furniture, and lighting are all custom-made. At the center of the home is a traditional chimney built from stone excavated from the site. The south-facing elevation opens fully to the sea, with four sets of full-height sliding glass doors enabling sublime views from the living areas, library, bathrooms, and the home's three suites. The north side, where the bunk rooms are located, is more enclosed, with rustic wooden shutters on the windows. The architecture expresses a deep respect for craftsmanship throughout, in the choice materials, design, and construction, turning a stay here into an unforgettable rural experience.

Robert Potter & Partners and Andy Stakes

CLIFFTOP HOUSE

2019 | Portpatrick, Scotland, UK

In a remote corner of Scotland's Southern Uplands, Clifftop House occupies the site of a former radar station used to monitor Cold War submarines—and it certainly looks like something straight out of a spy thriller. Planning permission had previously been refused for a more conventional house on the plot, and this design was the successful response: a single-story dwelling, burrowed into the cliffside with a turf roof, camouflaged brilliantly amid its harsh surroundings.

Extreme gales and rainstorms frequently batter the site, and thus reinforced concrete was chosen as a structural frame, with Caithness stone used for the walls; boulders excavated from the site were incorporated into the grass embankments hugging the building. Clifftop House is arranged in a cluster of south-facing rooms, connected by a glass passageway to the north. The entrance was also placed on the northern side to give protection from southerly winds. Uninterrupted glazing on the south side maximizes the sweeping views of the North Channel and takes advantage of solar gain to warm the house. An outdoor terrace was included to make the most of precious sunny days. Stone buttresses extend outward from the building, flanking the sides of each room to provide privacy for the inhabitants. Giving interiors as much attention as the exterior, the designers chose muted colors to harmonize with stone, grass, and sky, creating a homey, calm refuge in an otherwise rugged landscape.

The design of Kawakawa House deftly blends openness and concealment, shade and illumination. Located in Piha, a New Zealand seaside village on the rugged coast west of Auckland, it has an idyllic setting amid a dense grove of pohutukawa trees on a hillside close to the beach. Another two-story residence further down the slope obscured outlooks at the first-floor level, so the challenge for the design was to ensure that the home received enough light and could provide views of the sea.

The architects' solution was to raise it up on a concrete plinth and to reserve the lower, recessed level for a garage and parking area. Lifting the structure in this way also created a deliberate, intimate connection with the beautiful tree canopy. The upper level has a roughly square plan, with a small open-air courtyard in the center; the three bedrooms overlook forest, while the open-plan kitchen, dining, and living area is on the sea-facing side. Sliding glass doors paired with a woven-mesh balustrade enable uninterrupted sea views in the living area. The sloping roof allows both the living room and main bedroom to be double height. A continuous clerestory window wraps around the perimeter of the upper story, admitting sunlight and making the trees an emphatic visual presence in the house. A decor combining black steel elements with dark and pale timber cleverly echoes the natural interplay of light and shadow in the surrounding forest.

Alejandro Beautell
HOUSE IN TACORONTE
2017 | Tacoronte, Tenerife, Spain

Set on a rocky headland, this house in the city of Tacoronte on the island of Tenerife was once a traditional 1960s Spanish villa. Stark white with a terra-cotta hipped roof, it was badly maintained and crumbling on the exposed site. Tenerife-based architect Alejandro Beautell redesigned it as a sleek, modern fortress; maintaining the house's footprint, he topped it with a flat roof, gutted the interior, and completely remodeled the exterior using concrete. This somewhat austere finish protects the house from intense heat and wind, as well as visually referencing the island's dark volcanic landscape.

The main entrance sits within a smooth, striking two-toned facade pierced by square voids. Positioned on the second floor, the entryway leads to an open-plan kitchen, dining, and seating area with floor-to-ceiling glazing and mesmeric ocean views. Below this, the first floor serves as a shower room and lobby for a spacious terrace with an infinity pool, while the third floor contains three en suite bedrooms. In keeping with the exterior, the interiors maintain a stark, almost industrial aesthetic, with a staircase made of steel girders, walls inlaid with rock, and structural columns and beams in rough, board-formed concrete. The gardens have an equally spare design, featuring cacti and other hardy desert plants. It is not a cozy home—in Tenerife's hot climate, it does not need to be—but it is certainly arresting and utterly in tune with its stark environment.

OLD JAFFA HOUSE 3

2017 | Tel Aviv-Yafo, Israel

This extraordinary cavelike apartment is in the ancient port city of Jaffa (also known as Yafo), less than 2 miles (3.2 kilometers) south of Tel Aviv. Part of a network of centuries-old stone dwellings clinging to a hill, the sea-facing residence had grown organically over the years. It was originally made up of a series of individual rooms, each on its own floor, which were connected by steps and closed off by doors, resulting in a dark, labyrinthine space. Local practice Pitsou Kedem Architects transformed the apartment, bringing all the rooms onto the same level to create a sense of flow between them, and removing most internal doors, increasing light and opening up sea views.

Balancing an aesthetic that is at once modern and traditional, the firm covered the original ceiling decoration with white stucco, but removed the plaster covering the inside of the impressive domed roof above the kitchen in layers to expose the beautiful stone underneath. Elsewhere, arched walls and ceilings were painted white to illuminate the space as much as possible. Contrasting black tin detailing emphasizes doorways, window frames, furniture, and shelving. Now surprisingly open and spacious, the home includes a main bedroom, kitchen, dining room, living room, and outdoor terrace. It feels sleek, minimalist, and almost Art Deco in its aesthetic. Pops of bright color enliven the monochrome palette, and the eye is continuously drawn to the sea, its blues always framed by the apartment's curving lines.

HOUSE IN LOS VILOS

2020 | Los Vilos, Chile

Located on a wild, rocky promontory near the town of Los Vilos, Chile, this vacation house features a vast undulating roof that suggests both the waves of the Pacific and the shape of nearby mountains. Pritzker Prize–winning Ryue Nishizawa designed the residence as part of the Ochoalcubo project (see p. 158); its commanding and powerful presence stands almost in defiance of the untameable ocean beyond.

Supported by steel pillars and glazed walls on both sides, the roof's dramatic curves were formed by layering two types of concrete—slabs for the underside, left exposed as the house's ceiling, and poured concrete on top—with insulation board and waterproofing in between. At one point it dips down to ground level, dividing the space and concealing behind it a sauna with a sunken bath and sea views; elsewhere, arches define different areas for the dining room and kitchen, the living room, and a bedroom (separated by a partition wall). The main suite, meanwhile, is contained within a separate volume for privacy and peace. Burrowed into a cliff, and on a lower level, it connects to the main structure via a subterranean staircase. Timber floors and furniture, combined with the exposed-concrete ceiling, create a stripped-back, raw feel inside the home. But it is undoubtedly the roof that gives this house a unique sense of containment and flow, and connection with the primal landscape.

MS-DA and Johnson Naylor
RADAR
2019 | Dungeness, England, UK

This small house with twin pitched roofs can be found amid the unique shingle beach of Dungeness, a headland on England's southeastern coast. Its form echoes that of the two huts that were previously on the site, which served as a small testing station built by British manufacturer Decca Radar c.1961. At the compact vacation home, guests can experience the area's compelling blend of natural beauty and industrial architecture—the Dungeness A and B nuclear power stations sit on the horizon.

The cabin's corrugated-zinc cladding expresses a distinctive utilitarian aesthetic, while an oversize cylindrical chimney breaks the home's horizontal forms to create a strong visual profile. Defining a boundary with the rugged, open surroundings, the original concrete fence posts were retained by the architects for their sculptural value and as a nod to the cabin's past. Two decked terraces at the eastern and western ends of the house are designated for watching the spectacular Dungeness sunrises and sunsets, weather permitting. In response to the locale's changeable climate, the interior is seamless, snug, and protective, using a soft neutral palette and materials, such as pale herringbone brick for the flooring and whitewashed oak for the wall panels. A sauna room clad in raw hemlock slats, with views over the pebbled beach, provides a luxurious touch, as well as another place to shelter from the elements.

Belinda George Architects

MATAPOURI ROAD HOUSE

2019 | Tutukaka, New Zealand

Most coastal houses are all about views of the sea, but this summer retreat in New Zealand turns that expectation on its head. Matapouri Road House faces away from the cove below, instead overlooking a verdant area of bush. There were two reasons for this decision: firstly, there are obvious risks associated with clifftop building that both the client and architecture firm preferred to avoid. Secondly, this particular location held a strong emotional pull for the client, because as a child, sitting on a big palm leaf, he would slide down the site's steep slope toward those trees.

With its curving form, the house seems to wrap the site in a warm embrace. Set within a clearing and nestled against the hillside, the residence also has a sense of encampment and adventure. The C-shaped plan allows boundaries between the different interior spaces and their functions to dissolve: living, eating, and sleeping areas flow into one another, creating a relaxed vacation-home layout. Since the house is glazed on both sides, inhabitants can still catch glimpses of the sea down below as they move through the rooms. Connecting with the bush setting, timber is used in the main structure as well as inside to create a comforting, cocooning space; the aesthetic is homey, tactile, and calm. Exquisitely handcrafted furniture and textiles, and a muted decor with touches of bright color add to the home's deep sense of welcome.

Casa Ocho Quebradas comprises three concrete monoliths that seem to have been dropped into the landscape by cataclysmic forces. At the same time, its apparently random cantilevering and tilting forms suggest strength, solidity, and balance—something altogether more considered. Reflecting the local topography, Ocho Quebradas means "eight ravines," and the house is part of a wider project called Ochoalcubo ("eight cubed") initiated to mark the major earthquakes that affected Chile in 2010 and Japan in 2011. Following an extensive submissions phase, sixteen architecture studios, eight from each nation, were selected to design one house each on a wild strip of coast near the town of Los Vilos.

Protruding from the grassy slope, the lower horizontal volume offers panoramic views of the roiling sea below. This volume houses the communal areas and main bedroom, and at its heart is a jewellike glazed room containing a firepit; smoke siphons out of a towering concrete chimney above, another of the three monoliths. The chimney leans against the third part of the house, a four-story structure accommodating more bedrooms and a roof terrace. Interiors are decorated using pale textiles, weathered timber, and white marble to create a pleasing contrast with the rough gray concrete inside and out. Wooden planks used to pattern the concrete walls were recycled as shutters for the windows. The home's stark forms are a fitting response to their unforgiving coastal environment, but they also provide a tranquil escape that speaks of simple pleasures.

[3] BUILT TO EMBRACE THE OCEAN

The homes in this chapter are about as close to the ocean as one can live while remaining on dry land. In locations with generally calm seas, they enjoy plenty of sunshine and are on sites with gentle topographies: sheltered beaches and harbors, protective dunes, or low-lying rocks. They are a stroll from the shoreline, minutes from a swim, and the sound of breaking waves is ever present.

Characterized by openness and sensitivity to the landscape, these dwellings almost seem to reach out to the sea in an attempt to touch it. A Malibu hillside terrace cantilevers dramatically, its infinity pool appearing to be an extension of the boundless Pacific; a converted French fishing hut—once the starting point of ocean journeys—strips coastal living down to the essentials in order to fully embrace its environment; and the projecting wings of a Mexican beach residence appear like outstretched fingers gesturing toward the shore.

Transparency is key to these designs. In cool climates, this can mean vast spans of glazing—a Finnish coastal pavilion, for example, is contained by walls of glass, making the sea a permanent visual presence. For houses in warmer countries, glazing is all but unnecessary: sliding doors open to the elements, allowing boundaries between inside and outside to dissolve. Sometimes traditional methods of shading and ventilation using natural materials, such as Mexican *palapas* (open-sided palm-leaf shelters), are most effective, cleverly blended with more contemporary designs.

While the majority of buildings in this chapter extend horizontally with low profiles, a few reach skyward, such as a New Zealand retreat whose chimney-like light wells reference the shafts of disused gold mines nearby. And despite already being close to water, most bring it into their designs, with swimming pools, rock pools, and waterfalls.

Such gentle terrains are not without their challenges. Compromised views, rising sea levels, and planning laws are some of the hurdles that have been overcome to bring these homes into being. Fundamentally, what connects all these houses is their ability to usher residents into intimate communion with the ocean.

Shinichi Ogawa & Associates
SEASIDE VILLA
2017 | Hua Hin, Thailand

This weekend villa in the cosmopolitan Thai resort of Hua Hin enables an ideal balance between family time and cloistered privacy. With a prime position right on the beach, the ultraminimalist Zen palace replaced a previous property owned by the same clients. It consists of six cuboid self-contained "pods" made of white-painted concrete, one for each member of the family. Each of the pods has its own entrance, miniature courtyard, lounge area, and bathroom, and is glazed in the front and back to allow light to penetrate. (Frosted glass on the road-facing side creates privacy.) The pods also contain one or two sleeping areas, some concealed on mezzanines.

From the road at the rear of the property, the villa appears as six separate volumes. On the beach-facing side, however, it is united by a huge overhanging canopy that provides plenty of shade. The pods open out onto an expansive terrace with an infinity pool and a deck beyond. Communal areas include a dining and living area on the terrace, and a sauna, gym, and kitchen, housed in two separate buildings at the rear of the property. The interiors of the pods are brightly illuminated and utterly minimalist, with white walls and pale textiles. In this impressive and serene getaway, the shore is somewhere to leave the material things of life behind, to find space for oneself and yet enjoy the company of others.

SUMMER HOUSE

2016 | Southern Finland, Finland

This simple, beautifully crafted summer house in southern Finland fully embraces its coastal environment. Named "Kesäpaviljonki" (summer pavilion) in Finnish, the glass structure rests on an elevated stone plateau that stretches between a pine forest and the sea. Designed for a couple, the long, narrow volume features an open-plan living, kitchen, and dining area at one end and a bedroom at the other. Dividing these two spaces is a freestanding oak unit, which houses storage and a bathroom. Maximizing functionality and adding a touch of luxury, one external side of the unit integrates a concrete-lined nook fitted with a bathtub overlooking the water—an inviting spot to soak away stress.

A bladelike roof, which gently twists as well as ripples, mimics the curves of surrounding rock forms and the undulating waves of the sea. Deep roof overhangs provide protection from rain and sun, and decking that wraps around the entire house eases the transition from indoors to outdoors. Copper roof trim and earth-brown steel window frames and paneling add natural colors to the largely glazed facades, which give almost 360-degree views of the earth, sea, and sky. Inside, the ceiling is clad in battens of pale oak, giving the home a snug, almost boatlike feel, while the natural stone flooring makes a direct connection with the rocky outcrops outside. Subtle, serene, and filled with light from the midnight sun, the pavilion is a deeply restorative home surrounded by nature.

This home that Portland, Maine–based architecture firm Caleb Johnson Studio designed for a New York couple nearing retirement shows profound respect for the New England state's vernacular architecture, yet retains its own identity. The design incorporates the pitched roofs, sash windows, and timber cladding common to the area but reworks those elements into something contemporary.

The front of the house overlooks the sea, while the rear has views over wetlands. The main structure comprises two tall and elegant gabled volumes connected by a flat-roofed glazed passageway. To protect it from flooding, the house is raised aloft by pillars, which are in turn elevated on a concrete plinth; to optimize the use of space, the architects placed a carport and entrance lobby underneath the house. Inside, living areas, a bedroom, and a semi-open terrace facing the sea occupy the first floor, and the second floor houses three more bedrooms and two offices. To maximize views, the living room features expansive glazed sliding doors, and the office and bedroom windows wrap around the corners of the house. A pale cedarwood exterior harmonizes with the colors of the surrounding dunes, while the luminous, uncluttered interior employs a calming palette of sand, cream, gray, green, and blue, all colors found in the coastal and marshland environment. With its pure geometric forms and simple facades, In the Dunes House has an appeal that is both fresh and familiar.

LAND Arquitectos
ALMOST CUBE HOUSE
2017 | Pichilemu, Chile

Set against a barren coastal landscape of rocky cliffs and rolling surf, the sculptural forms of this Chilean house stand out dramatically. The area teems with nature—sea lions can often be glimpsed. This is the perfect location for connecting with the elements at their wildest. The starting point for the home's design was a cuboid (an "almost" cube) that has been stretched and pushed to create angled, undulating planes. Peaks in the roof raise the height above the kitchen-dining area and bedrooms to create a sense of openness, and the ceiling is supported by large V-shaped trusses that frame rather than obstruct views. To make the most of these panoramas, the home's living areas and three bedrooms have floor-to-ceiling glazing.

Casa Casi Cubo, as the residence is called in Spanish, is enveloped by a latticed pine pavilion, which takes the force of the strong local winds but still allows cooling ventilation to flow through the home's spaces. As the sun moves around the building, the screening casts abstract shadow patterns both outside and in, creating a cool, comfortable place to relax and to sense and savor the shifting moods of the day. The slatted skin also provides privacy for the bedroom areas. Throughout, there is an impression of unfurling, expansiveness, and ease that makes Almost Cube House a serene place to connect with nature.

VIKING

2017 | Fermanville, France

This diminutive beach house on the west coast of France takes its name from the siege of Viking invasions sustained by the site in the ninth century. It was originally a tiny 13 × 10 foot (4 × 3 meter) concrete fishing hut dating back to the 1950s. Planning regulations meant that the hut could not be added to in any way, but a restoration was allowed. The architects upgraded the exterior and roof, wrapping them in champagne-colored galvanized-metal cladding, and inserted two large windows with sliding glass panes into the facade to open the house up to the sea.

A surprising amount is packed into the interior. A bed tucks under the eaves on a new mezzanine floor; underneath this is a bathroom with shower, toilet, and sink. The rest of the downstairs space is an open-plan kitchen, living, and dining area. Up to eight people can fit around the dinner table; chairs by Icelandic designer Valdimar Harðarson fold flat and can be stowed away on wall hooks. The all-white interior has a fresh, light-hearted seaside vibe. Outside, there is a concrete terrace on which to eat or relax, and a tiny concrete barbecue. Viking is a place to enjoy a simpler life, yet it manages to achieve a purity of design and clever internal planning that outmatches many coastal cabins.

TE ARAI BEACH HOUSE

2020 | Te Arai, New Zealand

The key ideas underpinning this intelligently conceived and contextually sensitive house are simplicity, use of natural materials, and a commitment to fine craftsmanship. A pair of gabled timber sheds nestle amid pinewoods and sand dunes in an unspoiled area on the east coast of New Zealand's North Island. Their barnlike form references the rural architecture of the local area, and their presence feels modest, timeless, and benign.

Although simple, the house is far from bland or dull; it is crafted like a precious jewel, and its lines are knife sharp. The vertical lines of the timber cladding used on both walls and roofs echo the forms of nearby pine trees, and the wood's color will gradually blend in with the pale sand of the dunes as time passes. Sliding shutters in the facades allow air, light, and the amount of privacy to be adjusted as required. Nestled between the two buildings is a terrace and seating area warmed by an outdoor fireplace with a monolithic concrete chimney. Inside, alternating ceiling heights create a rhythm of expansive and cozy living areas. Wood is used throughout, on both floors and ceilings, creating a cosseting environment and a strong connection with the exterior, although the interior timber is oiled and therefore darker in tone. Exquisite stone facing, a concrete fireplace, and metal detailing complete the pure, stripped-back aesthetic. Te Arai Beach House lives in harmony with its fragile environment while retaining its own subtle individuality.

The unusual design of Casa Cal arose from a creative response to an awkward site. Part of a development of eight vacation homes near Mexico's surf capital, Puerto Escondido, the plot was set back from the beach, and first-floor views of the Pacific Ocean were blocked by the one-story dwellings in front.

Mexico City–based architecture firm BAAQ' therefore designed a two-story house—formed of two rectangular volumes arranged in an L-shape around a courtyard—in which the main bedroom and an outdoor living area that includes a terrace and pool is positioned on the second floor, while guest bedrooms are on the first. The swimming pool is contained within a concrete cube, which stretches up from first- to second-floor level to connect with the terrace; the living area is shaded by an open-sided traditional thatched palm-leaf shelter known as a *palapa*. Lining the main bedroom are louvered walls made from palm stems, chosen to create shifting shadow patterns. A white double-height external wall wraps around the north and west sides of the house, lending the building a bold, monolithic presence. The wall is intermittently pierced by cinder-blocks with decorative cutouts, which, along with sliding screen doors on the first floor, provide cross ventilation throughout the residence. Achieving a perfect fusion of solid volumes and voids, natural and man-made materials, and indoor and outdoor spaces, Casa Cal rises above its initial restrictions to become a soothing spot to enjoy ocean views and breezes.

Co Lateral
LYONS GARDEN HOUSE
2019 | Zihuatanejo, Mexico

Located in the resort city of Zihuatanejo, Mexico, Lyons Garden House taps into the restorative qualities of water and green space. The retreat is arranged in a U-shape around a garden courtyard: a lush lawned space bordered with tropical trees and shrubs. The central section of the house features two bedrooms and an office, with a shaded colonnade connecting to two wings—one set aside for dining, the other entirely devoted to meditation. Monumental without being heavy, the house has clean lines and solid forms made possible by the skilful use of concrete and tepetate, a volcanic soil found abundantly in Mexico.

The largest area of the house is the meditation wing: a vast room, devoid of any furniture, entered via a circular door. Here, the boundaries between inside and out are deliberately dissolved; entirely open at one end and with sliding glass doors on two sides, it houses a dreamlike pool that begins inside and then flows out and around the side of the building to face the sea. A flat concrete-slab roof with a deep overhang gives the space a ceremonial feel; a large circular skylight cuts through the roof, allowing in air, light, wind, and rain. An abstract arrangement of stepped concrete cubes demarcates the outdoor pool area, adding to the contemplative atmosphere. In full communion with nature, the house is a sublime place to find stillness.

Matthew Woodward Architecture
CRESCENT HOUSE
2018 | Sydney, NSW, Australia

A sophisticated response to a narrow, steeply sloping plot, Crescent House has a superb location overlooking Sydney Harbour. The clients were a young family that wanted a bright, well-lit home with various spaces to entertain and relax. They also wanted to make the most of the views. Matthew Woodward Architecture's design exceeds all of these ambitions, while unfolding in surprising ways that pay homage to the sea's changing rhythms and energy.

The three-story house consists of a pair of connecting rectangular volumes that step down the hill, but from the street it appears to be a single white volume set behind a garage. An unusual and important feature of the house is a large V-shaped void, cut out from the lower volume on its east side. This creates sinuous, airy double-height spaces, pulling in light and increasing sight lines between the home's living spaces. It also makes room for a steep sloping garden outdoors that feels like part of the indoor experience. Additional light wells are scattered around the house and concrete is used sculpturally on ceilings, walls, and floors, giving the house a flowing, organic feel. Opportunities to integrate green space are seized wherever possible: there is a lawn to the east and a pond to the west, and the main bedroom opens onto a garden on the roof. Perhaps thanks to its restrictions, Crescent House delivers something wholly original and perfectly in tune with its nautical context.

Situated on a strip of land between Mexico's Oaxacan mountains and the Pacific Ocean, Casa Cova is an imposing vacation home for a pair of families. Two long, slender wings are connected by a central common area, which faces out onto a spacious terrace with palm trees and a pool. The shared living space, with a high apex ceiling, is designed for entertaining and features a bar, dining room, kitchen, and lounge. It was constructed using local parota wood, and the roof is a traditional Mexican thatched *palapa* roof made with palm leaves. This provides shade and space for heat to escape through apertures at the top of the roof frame, cooling tropical temperatures to about 74 degrees Fahrenheit (23 degrees Celsius). The *palapa* provides a striking contrast with the board-formed concrete used for the rest of the structure, a material chosen for its ability to weather heat and wind. Natural breezes flow into the common area through the large lattice wall at the rear, which also creates patterns of light and shadow from dusk until dawn.

The two wings each consist of three rectangular concrete "pavilions" projecting out toward the beach, which contain three en suite bedrooms; the suites remain connected to each other via interlocking patios, which also provide cross ventilation and garden spaces. The home's organic material palette and strong linear patterns create a simple, soothing environment in which to enjoy the ocean setting.

Sometimes a few clever additions are all that are needed to optimize a home's coastal environment. In a beautiful setting on a tree-covered hillside in Malibu, California, this house has been transformed by architect Michael Goorevich and landscape architect Stephen Billings. The pair's ingenious interventions include a Modernist-inspired terrace with a swimming pool and pergola that together frame and maximize views of the Pacific, sky, and horizon.

In a design that pays homage to the horizontal forms of Californian Modernists such as Craig Ellwood and John Lautner, the L-shaped terrace, supported by black steel columns, cantilevers out toward the ocean, while the long, triangular, slanting pergola made from wood slats offers a cool, shaded space. The pergola's grid of battens stops halfway along one side of the terrace so that there is an exposed area in which to sunbathe or take in views of the ocean. The infinity pool stretches right to the terrace edge, creating the impression that the blue of the pool is continuous with that of the sea. Reflections of the clouds and sun bounce off the pool to create further optical effects that play with the boundaries of space. Sensitive landscaping, featuring native plants, creates a seamless connection between the garden and the natural landscape. Drawing upon the ocean's captivating unboundedness, this project dissolves the limits of architecture to create an elegant escape that is at one with its surroundings.

Every detail of these villas is designed to heighten the sensory experience of being close to the sea. This thoughtful development of three two-story houses occupies a superb site right next to the ocean in the town of Mui Ne, on Vietnam's southeastern coast. Elevated above the beach to ensure the best views and privacy, the three- and four-bedroom villas' connection with the outdoors is key to its design. The second floor of each house is set back in order to create spacious outdoor terraces level with the tops of palm trees, while main bedrooms on the first floor open directly to infinity pools and the ocean.

Floor-to-ceiling glazing in the living areas and bedrooms slides back to bring in breezes and frame views of the sea, sky, and horizon. To avoid distracting from the outlook, the decor is absolutely minimalist, with white walls, dark wood, and pale furniture. To the rear, where the bathrooms are located, slatted wood screening provides cross ventilation and shading. Landscaped gardens, planted with bamboo and banana trees, not only provide tropical green space, but also act as a sonic buffer between houses and road. Water is a constant theme throughout the villas, with plunge pools at the rear and ornamental ponds in the entrance halls of each house. All of these simple elements combine to create three utterly serene beachside retreats.

This cabana on Mexico's Michoacán coast is a discreet hideaway and the perfect place for drinks at sundown. Dug into a rocky cliff face above a beach and screened by vegetation, it is designed to blend into its natural surroundings as much as possible. The one-story building is purely intended for sunbathing, lounging, and simple meals: there is a shower room, and seating and dining areas, but no kitchen or bedrooms. These are in a main residence further along the hillside, reached by a shady path edged with palm trees, ferns, and other tropical plants.

The cabana's outdoor spaces include an expansive roof deck and two terraces further down the slope. An external staircase leads down to a skilfully camouflaged swimming pool: a basin hewn from rocks on the beach. The pool is partly lined with geometric tiles, although the surrounding rock is still left exposed in places, creating a seamless visual connection with the sea beyond. Plans to cover the cabana with a traditional Mexican thatched *palapa* roof were quickly jettisoned to avoid a clash with the site and to maintain the cabana's low-key ethos as well as providing a terrace for star-gazing. Abutting the cliff, the living room's back wall is clad in cuts of stone dug from the site, while red cedar paneling on the remaining walls, the ceiling, and that used in custom-built cabinetry is designed to capture a warm glow from the rays of the setting sun.

Johan Sundberg

SUMMERHOUSE H

2017 | Lilla Beddinge, Sweden

The strengths of this house's design are its simplicity, fine craftsmanship, and deep reverence for nature. Located in a conservation area on the Baltic Sea, Summerhouse H is set back from a narrow, tree-lined beach. It has a simple boxlike form, but its detailing lifts it far above the ordinary. A prominent chimney adds verticality, the roof pitches gently, and the porch has wind-shielding partitions that create a rhythm of open and closed spaces at the front of the house.

Bedrooms and bathrooms are positioned on one side of the building, and an open-plan living, kitchen, and dining area is on the other. The house's larch cladding is an important part of its calm, natural aesthetic: the wood's color blends in beautifully with the sandy earth and the green of the surrounding vegetation, and its surface is highly tactile. The silicone-treated larch is used in various ways on different elevations to create interesting visual effects. On the north facade, protruding battens have been attached in a girder-like formation to create patterns of light and shadow. On the southeastern, sea-facing elevation, slats are grouped in different-sized panels but all sit flush with one another. Interiors are simple, with white walls, more pale wood, and sheer curtains. A particular care and thoughtfulness are at the heart of the home's restful, modest beauty—it is a design that shows deep sensitivity for both its inhabitants and its surroundings.

Dumay Arquitectos
VC HOUSE
2018 | Huentelauquén, Chile

VC House is situated on a low-lying stretch of the north-central coast of Chile, amid an arid landscape pockmarked with scrub. On an exposed plot right next to the ocean, it delivers stunning views of the Pacific while shielding inhabitants from coastal winds and fierce sun in minimalist, stylish surroundings.

Slightly trapezoid on plan, the house is constructed from durable rough concrete and timber, apt choices for the wild surroundings. An expansive terrace facing the sea is covered with a bamboo roof, which casts pleasing abstract shadows throughout the day. Concrete walls at both ends act as windbreaks, but an opening has been made in one to keep the sea and landscape in sight. An interior courtyard with a firepit, accessible from the open-plan kitchen, living, and dining area, provides a second sheltered nook in which to relax. Floor-to-ceiling glazing on both sides of this living area provides views to the sea, while minimizing heat loss in the winter. Inside, pale wood on floors and ceilings complements the concrete exterior, while black timber detailing and black steel columns create bold contrast and give the house a restrained monochrome aesthetic. With a main bedroom, bunk room, and two bathrooms, plus a guest wing to one side, the house provides a sleek place to gather where the natural environment is the main event.

Crosson Architects

LIGHT MINE

2020 | Kuoatunu, New Zealand

With its eye-catching, abstract profile, Light Mine delivers an innovative take on the "bach"—the archetypal New Zealand vacation home. This award-winning house, which consists of three "pods" encircling a grassy courtyard, was designed for an extended family and can accommodate up to a dozen people. One pod with a living area and main bedroom faces the beach; the second, with a bunk room and another bedroom, connects to the first via a covered walkway. Across the courtyard is the third pod, a self-contained guest annex. The pyramidal light wells emerging from each of the pods give the property its distinctive silhouette. Inspired by the shafts in long-abandoned local gold mines, they flood the house with sunlight by day and yield views of the starlit sky by night. They also add a sense of a playfulness and mystery, encouraging closer inspection from both inside and out, and give the home a secure feeling of tentlike enclosure.

As well as gently subverting traditional bach architecture, Light Mine pays homage to it, with its single-story timber-clad structure and simple interior. Salvaged from a swamp, battens of silver-toned totara wood clad the exterior, enabling it to blend in with the surrounding sand dunes. Inside, a pale cedar used for the floor, walls, and furniture brightens the space and contrasts with the darker facade. A shining example of context-driven coastal architecture, Light Mine is both modest and wholly surprising.

Atelier Branco

CASA MÓDICO

2019 | São Miguel do Gostoso, Brazil

Casa Módico is a celebration of pure geometry, which uses a simple, archetypal form to create a serene seaside getaway. On the northeast coast of Brazil, it enjoys a superb beachside location, nestled amid gently undulating and scrubby dunes overlooking the Atlantic Ocean. The home consists of two white gable-roofed volumes separated by a narrow, walled courtyard; each one contains two en suite bedrooms. In the volume nearest the water is a living room furnished with only a large, double-sided sofa, where residents can gaze either at the ocean through a set of oversize glazed doors or across the courtyard into the neighboring volume. On the ocean-facing side, the doors open out onto a wide terrace, from which steps lead down to the beach. In the second volume is a kitchen, which opens out onto the courtyard, where there is a long dining table of weathered wood. The white-painted terra-cotta-tiled roofs are invisible from the houses' gable ends, as they are hidden by pediments that give the two volumes a crisp profile. Inside, however, the roof tiles are exposed to create a textured ceiling, crisscrossed by battens and beams. Doorways positioned at exactly the same points in both houses allow cross ventilation, as do sections of lattice brickwork in the walls between private and public internal areas. Although bold within the soft dune landscape, the pristine volumes of Casa Módico never seem to unduly compete with it.

ST ANDREWS BEACH VILLA

2019 | St Andrews Beach, VIC, Australia

An example of "slow building," this house has been added to and remodeled over the course of twenty years as its owners' needs have changed and the weather has worn it out. Overlooking the Bass Strait, the strait that separates Australia and Tasmania, the villa is subjected to strong sun, ferocious winds, and rain. Work took place in three phases: the first was the building of two linked volumes on pilotis, one for sleeping and one for living, with a deck and full-width staircase leading from the main entrance down to the sand. The second was the addition of a huge elevated terrace perpendicular to the house, with a lap pool and cabana. Finally, the space under the house and the staircase was adapted to add four bedrooms and a greenhouse complete with a gravel garden, creating a cool, shaded, and entirely protected space.

The house is clad in jarrah-wood rainscreens that pivot and fold to admit northern light. They have weathered over time to blend in with the surroundings. Inside, worn or rusted elements were reused, forming a key part of the interior design: steel panels became wall surfaces; distressed timber was recycled in joinery throughout; and steel-plate handrails were fashioned into folding library tables and containers for firewood. Over time, the home's own decay has become part of its very fabric, in a gradual process of adaptation and renewal.

Casa Naila marries flexible family accommodations with a strikingly abstract design. It shows great sensitivity to its surroundings: a rocky, wild patch of coast in the Mexican state of Oaxaca. Built on a raised concrete platform, the residence consists of four pitched-roof volumes, which cluster around a cross-shaped courtyard containing garden, swimming pool, and outdoor dining area. Designed with communal living in mind, the house is able to accommodate up to fifteen people, and because of its village-like layout, it manages to achieve an easygoing balance between private and public spaces. The volumes are built from relatively low-cost materials—concrete and palm bone wood, locally available and widely used—creating a durable modern house that blends into its coastal environment. One volume houses the kitchen and a bedroom upstairs; a second serves as an indoor living room; the third one has bedrooms on both floors; and the fourth is a studio apartment. Facades, which have barnlike doors and shutters, change in visual character as they are opened up or secured closed. Seascapes are visible from every room—and looking back from the beach, Casa Naila presents ever-shifting sculptural and textured forms to passersby. The house has no perimeter fencing, so it merges with the beach area; visitors to the beach are free to use the pool and courtyard. Relaxed and rustic yet contemporary, this is a home with an open, welcoming ethos.

INDEX

Page numbers in **bold** refer to illustrations.

[1] BUILT WITHIN THE OCEAN

Photographer Jesper Anhede, anhede.se: 40, 42; Pirak Anurakyawachon: 60, 61, 62, 63; David Barbour: 78, 79; Danny Bright: 16, 17, 18, 19; DECA Architecture: 54, 55; © Simon Devitt: 80, 81, 82, 83; Thibault Dini: 20, 21, 22, 23; Yiorgos Kordakis: 25, 27, 28, 29, 34, 35, 36, 37, 38, 39; Åke E:son Lindman: 24; The Manta Resort, Pemba Island: 41, 43; George Messaritakis: 56, 57, 58, 59; Justin Nicholas: 10, 11, 12, 13, 14; Ema Peter: 64, 65, 66, 67; Raad: 50, 51, 52, 53; Nigel Rigden: 74, 75, 76, 77; Photos: Jason Schmidt: 68, 69, 70, 71, 72, 73; Sato Shinichi: 30, 31, 32, 33; Ken'ichi Suzuki: 44, 45, 46, 47, 48, 49.

[2] BUILT TO CONFRONT THE OCEAN

Alejandro Beautell, architect / Jose Oller, photographer: 134, 135, 136, 137; Patrick Bingham Hall: 112, 113, 114, 115; Billy Bolton: 148, 149, 150, 151; © Simon Devitt: 120, 121, 122, 124, 125, 152, 153, 155, 156, 157; William Eckersley: 104, 106, 107; Pezo von Ellrichshausen: 88, 89, 90, 91, 92, 93; Roland Halbe: 108, 109, 110, 111; Architecture: Pitsou Kedem Architects / Photography: Amit Geron: 138, 139, 140, 141; Photographer: Michael Nicholson: 116, 117, 118, 119; © Cristóbal Palma: 142, 143, 145, 146, 147, 158, 159, 160, 161; Robert Potter & Partners and Andy Stakes / Douglas Gibb: 126, 127, 128, 129; © Patrick Reynolds: 130, 131, 132, 133; Rachael Smith Photography: 105; Bent Raanes Sørensen: 94, 95, 96, 97; Derek Swalwell: 98, 99, 100, 101, 102, 103.

[3] BUILT TO EMBRACE THE OCEAN

Anonimous Principal: Alfonso Jimenez, Anonimous CDMX: Bárbara Trujillo, Architecture Team: Mónica Ochoa, Francisco Martínez, Ana Cristina Fernández, Lucrecia Brero, Joaquín Ríos, Media & Marketing: María Luisa Guzmán, Construction: Juan Carlos Steffanoni, Developer: ASARI, Landscape Design: Fritz Sigg / AMBIENTE ARQUITECTOS, Lighting Design: Martin Leal / LAMPE / Photography: Rafael Gamo: 206, 207, 208, 209, 211; Pirak Anurakyawachon: 166, 167, 168, 169; Trent Bell: 174, 175, 176, 177, 192, 193, 194, 195; Federico Cairoli: 238, 239, 240, 241; Jules Couartou: 182, 183, 184, 185, 186, 187; © Simon Devitt: 234, 235, 236, 237; Murray Fredericks Photography: 202, 203, 204, 205; Rory Gardiner & Lorena Darquea: 220, 221, 222, 223, 224, 225; Michael Goorevich, Architect, Brian Guizot, Contractor, Stephen Perlof, Structural Engineer, Stephen Billings, Landscape Architect, Eric Staudenmaier, photographer: 212, 213, 214, 215; Oki Hiroyuki: 216, 217, 218, 219; Mika Huisman/ Decopic: 170, 171, 172, 173; Ignacio Infante Cobo: 230, 231, 232, 233; LAND Arquitectos: Cristobal Valenzuela H., Angela Delorenzo A., Javier Lorenzo / Sergio Pirrone: 178, 179, 180, 181; Trevor Mein: 242, 243, 244, 245; Camilo Moreno Oliveros, Héctor Campagna Oliveros, Daniel Moreno Ahuja and Interior Design by LIA – Laboratorio de Interiorismo y Apropiación: 196, 197, 199, 200, 201; Edmund Sumner: 246, 247, 248, 249, 250, 251; Chief Architect Johan Sundberg, Associate Architects Itziar del Río Gómiz, Henrik Ålund, Structural Engineer Sven-Göran Svensson (SG Svensson AB), Contractor Roland Sjöholm (SA Bygg AB), Builders Roland Sjöholm, Stefan Andersson, Photography Markus Linderoth: 226, 227, 228, 229; Simon Wilson (photographer), Sonia Hawkins (interiors): 188, 189, 190, 191.

Cover photo: Justin Nicholas

Phaidon Press Limited
2 Cooperage Yard
London E15 2QR

Phaidon Press Inc.
65 Bleecker Street
New York, NY 10012

phaidon.com

First published 2021

ISBN 978 1 83866 327 8

A CIP catalogue record for this book is available from the British Library and the Library of Congress.

Commissioning Editor: Emilia Terragni
Project Editors: Emma Barton and Robyn Taylor
Production Controller: Gif Jittiwutikarn
Design: SJG / Joost Grootens, Dimitri Jeannottat,
Julie da Silva
Text: Rachel Giles

Printed in China

The publisher would like to thank Jane Birch, Vanessa Bird, Lisa Delgado, and Rosie Pickles for their contributions to the book.